Nature's Children

TERMITES

Jen Green

GROLIER

FACTS IN BRIEF

Classification of Termites

Class:	*Insecta* (insects)
Order:	*Isoptera* (termites: a word that means "equal wing")
Family:	Five families: *Mastotermitidae*, *Hodotermitidae*, *Kalotermitidae*, *Rhinotermitidae*, and *Termitidae*.
Genus:	There are 285 genera of termites.
Species:	There are 2,500 species of termites.

World distribution.   All continents except Antarctica. Mainly in tropical regions.

Habitat.   Varied, including forests and dry grasslands.

Distinctive physical characteristics.   Small, pale, thick-bodied insects with large heads, generally wingless. Young kings and queens have two pairs of wings.

Habits.   Live in colonies that cooperate to find food and rear young. Most termites live underground.

Diet.   Wood, dung, and plant matter in the soil. These insects can become destructive pests.

© 2004 The Brown Reference Group plc
Printed and bound in U.S.A.
Edited by John Farndon and Angela Koo

Published by:

**An imprint of Scholastic
Library Publishing
Old Sherman Turnpike, Danbury,
Connecticut 06816**

Library of Congress Cataloging-in-Publication Data

Green, Jen.
  Termites / Jen Green.
    p. cm. — (Nature's children)
  Includes index.
  Summary: Describes the physical characteristics, habits, and habitats of termites.
  ISBN 0–7172–5957–9 (set)   ISBN 0–7172–5960–9
  1. Termites—Juvenile literature. [1. Termites.] I. Title. II. Series.

QL529.G74 2004
595.7'36—dc21

                                                      2003049179

Contents

Termites are insects, like beetles, bees, and butterflies. But termites are not just any insects. Unlike most insects, they live in gigantic groups called colonies. A colony of termites is really one big family—the world's biggest. Up to five million live in a colony, all working together to keep things going.

Termites aren't pretty like butterflies, but they do have one amazing talent—they are very skillful builders. Most human families don't build their own home, but termites do. What's more, in relation to their size, their homes are the largest of any animal.

Termites often build themselves huge towering nests made of clay glued together by the insects' saliva.

What Are Termites?

Termites live in hot, tropical regions in Australia, Africa, and South America. They live in many different landscapes, including lush, green forests and rolling grasslands. The only places they never live are really cold places such as the Arctic, because there is no food for them there.

Termites form a large group, or "order," of insects. Amazingly enough, the termite order contains over 2,800 species (types). And there are huge numbers of every type of termite living around the world. Over 50 different species of termite are found in the United States alone.

Termites are sometimes called "white ants" because like ants, they live in large colonies under the ground. However, termites aren't closely related to ants. Their closest relatives are cockroaches and praying mantises.

Look closely at these termites, and you see the three body sections: the head, a whiter thorax, and the abdomen.

Body Shape

Like all insects, termites have six nimble legs that they use for running and climbing. Like other insects, too, termites' bodies are divided into three main parts. They have a head, a middle part called a thorax, and a rear part called an abdomen. The head carries the mouth and the insect's "feelers," or antennae. The legs are attached to the thorax. The abdomen is divided into several sections.

But while most insects have two pairs of wings, most termites have none. Some termites do grow wings at one stage in their lives, but even then they are poor fliers.

Most insects also have a tough outer skin like a shell. Termites are different—their bodies are generally quite soft and squashy, though they have hard heads.

No Place Like Home

Termite colonies contain huge numbers of insects—often over a thousand and up to five million. That's as many insects as there are people living in a big city! All the termites in a colony belong to just one family, with a mother, father, and thousands of children. Colonies like these are found in warm places all around the world.

Termites build the most elaborate homes of any insect. Most species live underground. Some termites dig out a large, cavelike nest in the soil, topped by a tower that may rise 20 feet (6 meters) in the air! Compared to the termites' size, they are far taller than the highest skyscrapers built by people. The tall towers, made of baked earth, work as chimneys, funneling warm air out of the nest.

Termite nests in the tropical grasslands of Kenya in Africa often have spectacular pinnacles.

Different Roles

Not all termites are identical. Every colony contains several different types of termite. These types are called castes, and each has a different job to do.

There is one mother, called the queen. Her job is to lay eggs that hatch into young insects. The queen's eggs are fertilized by a father-termite called the king, who lives by her side. All the other insects belong to two more castes. They are either workers or soldiers. The workers carry out all sorts of tasks, while soldiers have just one role—to defend the nest.

Termite soldiers with their large jaws stand guard while smaller, paler workers repair a tunnel.

King and Queen

The king and queen are the parents of all the other termites in the nest. They look very different from their children. For a start, they are the only termites that have eyes and can see—and also the only ones with wings. They are much larger, too. The king is a well-developed insect that may be twice the size of an ordinary worker. But even he is dwarfed by his giant mate, the queen.

The queen is a strange-looking insect, resembling a plump sausage. That is because the rear part of her body is swollen with thousands of eggs. Some termite queens lay an amazing 30,000 eggs in a single day—that's one every few seconds. As soon as the eggs are laid, the workers carry them away. The king and queen live all the time in a special chamber at the heart of the nest. They rarely, if ever, come out. They are faithful to one another and never part.

The abdomen of this queen termite is so enlarged
with eggs that you can hardly see her tiny head.

Hard Workers

Besides the king and queen, there are countless blind worker termites in the colony. Workers are the smallest adult termites. They may be either male or female. But their bodies remain undeveloped, so they cannot breed. They have no wings, so they cannot fly; but they can crawl along the ground, climb trees, and burrow through the soil.

Worker termites are responsible for all the day-to-day running of the colony. They gather food, build and repair the nest, and clean and feed all the other termites. They act as hunters, nursemaids, messengers, builders, miners, and cleaners all rolled into one.

A big column of worker termites crawls down the side of a tree after finding some food.

A Soldier's Life

Unlike a worker termite, a soldier has just one job. A soldier termite's role is to defend the colony—with its own life if necessary. Soldier termites also guard the lines of workers leaving the nest and returning with food.

Like human soldiers, soldier termites have armor and weapons that help them fight. Their bodies are fairly soft, but they have tough legs and large heads strengthened with a hard outer skin. Some soldiers have large, fierce jaws to bite their enemies. Others have slender snouts shaped like nozzles that squirt sticky poison at their foes.

Like worker termites, soldiers are blind. But they can detect their enemies by smell and touch, using their long antennae.

The effectiveness of the soldier termite's jaws are clearly shown as this one nips a man's finger.

This closeup shows how the queen termite's head and thorax emerge from her gigantic abdomen.

Communication

Termite societies run smoothly as clockwork all the time. Every termite knows exactly what to do and does it without question. They know because they communicate well. Of course, termites don't communicate by talking. Instead, messages are passed using scent, taste, and touch.

The queen communicates with the other termites by releasing special scents from glands in her skin. The workers lick these scents off her body as they clean her, then pass them on to others in their food. Different scents may tell termites in the colony where to find food, when to mate (or not), or whether to become a soldier or a worker. Outside the nest the blind workers identify one another by scent and touch. Termites that belong to a rival nest have a different smell, so workers and soldiers may attack them.

Master Builders

This is a nest of tree termites. The nest is usually round, but this one has been broken by the photographer to reveal the insects and their passages inside

Termites are the master builders of the insect world. Some species live high in trees, in round nests made of chewed wood fibers. This mixture works like papier-mâché. It is soft and flexible when it's moist, but rock-hard when it's dry.

Most termites live underground, in nests topped by tall ventilation chimneys. The nests are made of tiny pellets of soil or sand stuck together with the termites' saliva and their own feces. They are very hard on the outside—so hard that people sometimes climb them to see the view from the top!

As warm air escapes from the chimney, cool air is drawn in below. That keeps the nest at just the right temperature. The workers open or close openings inside the chimney with mud to fine-tune the temperature of the nest.

Unusual Nests

In Africa some types of forest-dwelling termites build unusual nests. Instead of chimneys, they are topped with large caps shaped like mushrooms. These caps are made of hardened mud, and there may be more than five of them piled on top of one another! In the lush forests where these termites live, rain falls nearly every day. The mushroom caps act as umbrellas to keep rain out of the nest.

In the Australian Outback, where the weather is hot and dry, some termites build unusual flat-sided chimneys. These chimneys have two broad faces that always point east and west. They also have two narrow sides that point north and south. At dawn and dusk the sun is low in the sky and warms the broad sides of the chimneys. This heats the nest below. At midday the sun is very fierce but very high in the sky. So only a narrow edge faces the sun. That keeps the nest cool.

Opposite page:
It can be very rainy in tropical forests. So some termites build mushroom caps in layers piled one on top of the other to keep the rain off.

25

Inside the Nest

Underneath its cap of hardened mud a termite nest is honeycombed with little caves, like a miniature underground city. A maze of narrow passages leads to rooms, or "chambers," where the termites live and work. The king and queen live in a large cave called the royal chamber. There they are fed and cleaned by the workers. The eggs and young are reared in rooms called nurseries. The nests of some termites even contain strange underground gardens where the termites grow their food.

Underneath the nest is a network of tunnels leading down into the earth for 30 feet (10 meters) or more. The workers dig these shafts to reach water sources deep below. They also help with drainage if rainwater enters the nest.

Termite Trails

Just as roads radiate out from major cities, so a network of little trails fans out from a termite nest. They spread out far and wide around the nest, often hundreds of yards long.

Every day thousands of workers crawl back and forth along these little roads, bringing food and water to the nest.

Many termite trails lie underground. Others are hollowed out of rotting wood. Where the trails run above ground, the clever little builders roof them in with mud. That is because termites don't like to be exposed to bright light. Where termite trails appear above ground, a huge mass of moving insects can be seen. Streams of insects mingle, with some going in one direction, some in the other.

This is a fungus garden inside a termite's nest,
where the insects tend the fungus for them to eat.

A Bite to Eat

Most termites eat certain kinds of plant food, including rotting wood, rotting plant matter in the soil, dead leaves, dead grass, and old roots.

Wood and other plants are made of a stringy material called cellulose. Cellulose is hard for animals to digest. But termites have some help. Inside their guts live tiny creatures called protozoans that are far too small for us to see. They may be small, but they can break down the tough cellulose. That helps termites digest their food.

Remarkably, termites can use the energy they get from cellulose to eat another kind of food—thin air! Termites are the only animals that can actually feed on the nitrogen gas that makes up 78 percent of the air.

Some termites grow their own food—a kind of fungus (like a mushroom). The fungus is grown deep inside the termite nest, in special chambers called fungus gardens. Worker termites bring shredded leaves to nourish the fungus and then feed on it as it grows.

Young Termites

Some young insects, such as butterflies, look very different from adults when they hatch. But baby termites hatch out as miniversions of the adults, only without wings. These baby termites adults are called larvae. They are so helpless they must be fed by their parents or their brothers and sisters.

Each baby termite, or larva, could grow up to become a worker or a soldier. Or it could turn into a young termite called a nymph. Nymphs eventually sprout wings and fly away to start a colony of their own. Some nymphs have wing pads that could grow into wings, but don't grow because the king and queen keep biting them. The king and queen do that to keep some of them from flying away. That makes sure that enough grow up to be workers. Termites like them are called false workers, or pseudergates (said SUE-der-gates).

New Nest Makers

At certain times of year a new caste of young termites grows up in the nest. They have dark bodies and well-developed heads with large eyes. Unlike other termites, they have two pairs of long, gauzy wings. These unusual termites are young kings and queens—the special termites that can fly away to mate and start new nests. They are called alates.

Alates are weak fliers. So they crawl some way above ground before flying off. Alates emerge from other colonies at the same time. So they need only fly a short way before landing to find a mate and snapping off their wings. The alates do a brief run to court each other, then mate. Each pair of insects finds a beetle hole or digs a small nest in the soil and starts to breed there. And so a new colony is established. In time the tall towers of new nests rise above ground.

Opposite page: Alates gather on a tree trunk before launching themselves into the air to search for mates from other nests.

Sworn Enemies

Termites have many enemies in the animal kingdom. They provide a nourishing meal for all sorts of animals, including frogs, lizards, mammals, and many kinds of birds.

In Asia termites are eaten by the long-nosed pangolin. In both North and South America sticky-tongued armadillos hunt termites in grasslands, and sharp-clawed anteaters catch them in forests. In South Africa the same job is done by the long-snouted aardvark and in Australia by the spiny echidna.

All these mammals are well equipped to break into termites' nests. Their strong, sharp claws can rip through the hard, baked mud of the termite chimneys. They also have slender snouts with long, sticky tongues designed to slurp up insects.

The birds that feed on termites have the right gear, too—long, curved beaks that probe into the nests. Frogs such as poison dart frogs can wait until they come out—then lick them up with their long tongues.

A raiding party of Matabele ants marches into a termites' nest and grabs some termite workers to eat.

38

Minifriends and Foes

Besides large enemies such as birds and anteaters, termites have small foes that are just as dangerous. Their archenemies are army ants. They are fierce, meat-eating ants that march through the forest in huge numbers, killing any creature they find. Unlike termites' other enemies, ants are small enough to march right into their nests. Groups of army ants sometimes raid termite nests to steal the eggs and young.

Not all other insects are enemies. Some insects live with termites in peaceful harmony. Tiny beetles live in some termite nests as permanent guests. They are fed by the termites. In return they ooze a liquid that the termites feed on. This helping relationship between creatures is called symbiosis.

Pesky Insects

Opposite page: *This picture shows the kind of damage termites can do to woodwork when they get their teeth into it.*

People see termites as pests because they munch wood and paper. They can easily destroy books, furniture, and even the timber framework of houses. They burrow deep into old wood and eat from the inside outward, leaving just the painted surface. Often the damage isn't discovered until too late.

Where buildings have wooden foundations, termites can eat away underneath and bring everything crashing down. They also cause chaos by chewing up wooden railroad ties. People sometimes build expensive metal foundations and steel railroad ties to beat the termites. The insects also nibble crops and fruit trees.

All this makes them public enemy number one! People wage war on termites by destroying their nests. They also soak timbers in chemicals that poison the termites. But termites are very difficult to get rid of once they move in.

A Helping Hand

Although many people see termites as pests, they can be a great help. They play a vital role in the life of the forests, grasslands, and deserts where they live. By eating plants, they help break down the nourishment plants contain. It returns to fertilize, or enrich, the soil so that more plants can grow.

Termites also provide food for many other creatures, from tiny ants to birds, reptiles, mammals, and even humans. In some hot countries these insects are actually a delicacy! They provide a source of much-needed protein in human diets when other foods are scarce.

People in Botswana in Africa like frying up winged termites for a tasty meal with a crunchy texture.

Termites in the Past

Opposite page:
These termites are perfectly preserved in amber—the once-sticky tree sap that trapped them 35 million years ago. The darker circles are tiny air bubbles.

Termites are a very ancient group of insects. Experts believe they were one of the first types of insects to develop on Earth—over 200 million years ago. They crawled around the same forests as dinosaurs. Yet when the dinosaurs died out around 65 million years ago, the termites survived. We humans appeared little more than 100,000 years ago.

How do we know that termites lived so long ago? Their bodies are too small and fragile to last like huge dinosaur bones. But sometimes termite remains have been preserved in a precious stone called amber. Amber is made from tree sap that oozed from trees, then turned to stone millions of years ago. Long ago, termites crawling on the trees were trapped in this sticky sap. The sap then slowly hardened to become amber, perfectly preserving the bodies of the trapped insects.

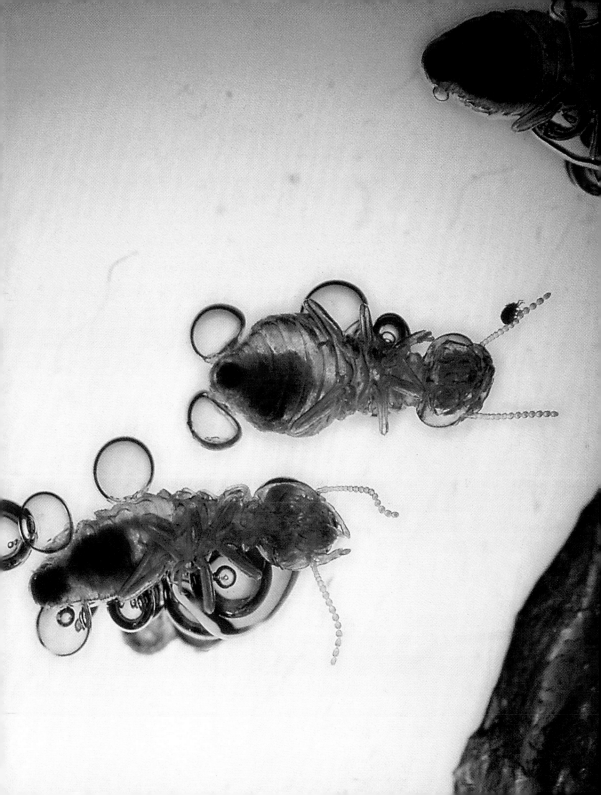

Other Social Insects

Termites are not the only insects to have a social life. Ants and some kinds of wasps and bees live in colonies too. All these social insects are quite closely related to each other—but not to termites. Their nests work in different ways than termite colonies.

Ant, wasp, and bee colonies contain a queen, large numbers of workers who do all the daily chores, and sometimes soldiers. But all the workers and soldiers are female—unlike in a termite nest. In ant, wasp, and bee colonies males are only reared at certain times of year to mate with the young queens. They die soon after mating, so there is no king. All the insects in the nest are the queen's children, so the colony is an overgrown family run by a single mother. Some ant colonies contain several queens, but still no king.

Words to Know

Abdomen The rear section of an insect's body.

Amber A precious stone made from hardened tree sap.

Antenna (plural antennae) The long projections, or "feelers," on an insect's head that help it sense the world.

Caste A particular type of insect in the termite colony with a certain job to do.

Cellulose A tough material that forms the walls of plant cells (and is difficult for plant-eating animals to digest).

Colony A group of animals that live together and cooperate to find food and rear their young.

Gut Part of the digestive system of an animal where nourishment from food is absorbed.

King The fertile male insect in a termite colony whose job is to fertilize the eggs.

Nymph The young of an insect such as a termite. A termite nymph has wing pads and will grow to be a winged adult.

Queen The fertile female insect in a termite colony, whose job is to lay eggs.

Species A particular type of animal.

Thorax The middle section of an insect's body, which carries the legs and the wings if present.

INDEX

Cover Photo: Bruce Coleman: Alain Compost
Photo Credits: Ardea: Clem Haagner 26, 33, Ingrid Van den Berg 11; NHPA: Mark Bowler 4, 34, Nigel J. Dennis 7, 8, 21, 30, 41, 45, Andy Rouse 22, Anne & Steve Toon 29; Oxford Scientific Films: Tim Jackson 37, David Macdonald 12, 15, 38, 42; Photodisc: Jeremy Woodhouse 25; Still Pictures: Nigel J. Dennis 18/19.